A Day in the Life: Desert Animals

Meerkat

Anita Ganeri

Heinemann
LIBRARY

Chicago, Illinois

www.heinemannraintree.com
Visit our website to find out
more information about
Heinemann-Raintree books.

To order:
☎ Phone 888-454-2279
▣ Visit www.heinemannraintree.com
to browse our catalog and order online.

Edited by Daniel Nunn, Rebecca Rissman, and Sian Smith
Designed by Richard Parker
Picture research by Elizabeth Alexander
Production by Victoria Fitzgerald
Originated by Capstone Global Library Ltd
Printed and bound in China by South China Printing
 Company Ltd

14 13 12 11 10
10 9 8 7 6 5 4 3 2 1

**Library of Congress Cataloging-in-
Publication Data**
Ganeri, Anita, 1961–
 Meerkat / Anita Ganeri.
  p. cm. — (A day in the life. Desert animals)
 Includes bibliographical references and index.
 ISBN 978-1-4329-4773-6 (hc)
 ISBN 978-1-4329-4782-8 (pb)
 1. Meerkat—Juvenile literature. I. Title.
 QL737.C235G36 2011
 599.74'2—dc22   2010022821

Acknowledgments
The author and publisher are grateful to the following
for permission to reproduce copyright material: Alamy
pp. 13 (© WorldFoto/Alamy), 21 (© AfriPics.com/
Alamy); Carolyn Ireland p. 16; Corbis pp. 4, 14, 23
glossary groom, 23 glossary mammal (© Paul A. Souders);
FLPA pp. 7, 23 glossary burrow (© Mark Newman),
8, 15 (© Vincent Grafhorst/Minden Pictures), 17 (©
Shem Compion); iStockphoto p. 5 (© Els van der Gun);
Photolibrary pp. 9 (Peter Arnold Images/Martin Harvey),
11 (Mark Newman/Superstock), 12 (David Macdonald/
OSF), 20 (Gunter Ziesler/Peter Arnold Images), 23
glossary poison (David Macdonald/OSF); Shutterstock
pp. 10, 23 glossary desert (© Karol Kozlowski), 18, 19, 23
glossary predator (© EcoPrint), 22, 23 glossary claw
(© Pyshnyy Maxim Vjacheslavovich), 23 glossary insect
(© Anke van Wyk).

Front cover photograph of a suricate or meerkat (Suricata
suricatta) family, in the Kalahari Desert, South Africa,
reproduced with permission of Shutterstock (© EcoPrint).

Back cover photograph of (left) a meerkat with pups
reproduced with permission of Corbis (© Paul Souders);
and (right) a suricate or meerkat (Suricata suricatta)
standing on guard, reproduced with permission of
Shutterstock (© EcoPrint).

We would like to thank Michael Bright for his assistance in
the preparation of this book.

Contents

Some words are shown in bold, **like this**.
You can find them in the glossary on page 23.

What Is a Meerkat?

A meerkat is a **mammal**.

All mammals have some hair on their bodies and feed their babies milk.

mongoose

Meerkats are about the size of large squirrels.

They belong to a group of mammals called mongooses.

Where Do Meerkats Live?

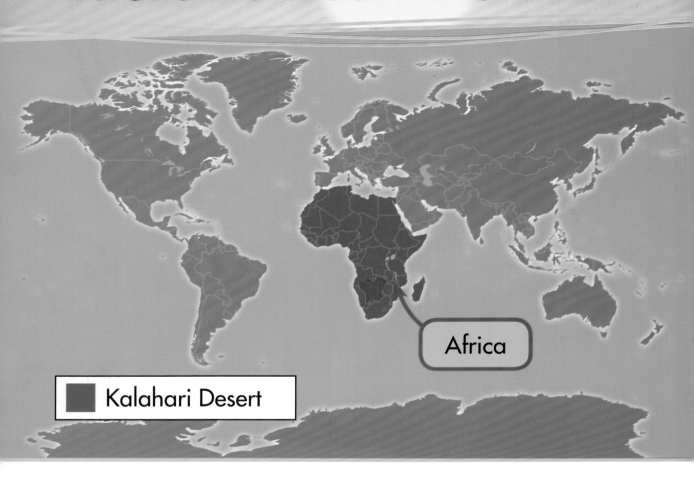

Africa

Kalahari Desert

Meerkats live in the Kalahari **Desert** in southern Africa.

It is hot and dry in the desert.

burrow

A lot of the desert is covered in sand.

The meerkats dig **burrows** in the sand or live in burrows dug by other animals.

What Do Meerkats Look Like?

claws

tail

Meerkats have long, thin bodies, covered in brown-gray fur.

They have large dark patches around their eyes.

Meerkats have long **claws** on their front feet for digging.

They use their tails for balancing when they are standing upright.

What Do Meerkats Do During the Day?

Meerkats come out of their **burrows** in the morning.

Then they lie in the sun to warm up.

Meerkats spend most of the day looking for food.

If it gets too hot, they take shelter in their burrows or under a bush.

What Do Meerkats Eat?

scorpion

Meerkats can eat scorpions without being harmed by their **poison**.

They also eat **desert insects**.

Meerkats can live without drinking water.

They get the water they need from eating desert plants and animals.

Do Meerkats Live in Groups?

Meerkats live in large groups of up to 30 animals.

During the day, the meerkats **groom** each other and play together.

burrow

Each group lives in its own **burrow**.

The burrows have long tunnels with many entrance and exit holes.

Where Are Baby Meerkats Born?

Baby meerkats are born in the **burrows**.

During the day, other females in the group look after them while their mother hunts for food.

The babies go outside for the first time when they are four weeks old.

Their mother teaches them what kind of food to eat.

Does Anything Hunt Meerkats?

jackal

While meerkats are outside during the day, they have to look out for **predators**.

Jackals, eagles, and falcons like to hunt and eat meerkats.

The meerkats take turns standing guard.

If the guard sees danger, it barks or whistles, and the meerkats then run back into their **burrows**.

What Do Meerkats Do at Night?

In the evening, it gets cold in the **desert**.

The meerkats stop feeding and go back into their **burrows** to sleep.

The meerkats only come out of their burrows the next morning if it is warm and sunny.

If it is rainy or cloudy, they stay inside.

Meerkat Body Map

Glossary

 **burrow** hole in the ground where a meerkat lives

 **claw** sharp, nail-like part of a meerkat's feet

 **desert** very dry place that is rocky, stony, or sandy

 **groom** clean each other's fur

 **insect** animal that has six legs, such as a grasshopper

 **mammal** animal that feeds its babies milk. All mammals have some hair or fur on their bodies.

 **poison** something that can cause illness or death

 **predator** animal that hunts other animals for food

Find Out More

Books

Haldane, Elizabeth. *Desert: Around the Clock with the Animals of the Desert* (24 Hours). New York: Dorling Kindersley, 2006.

Hodge, Deborah. *Desert Animals* (Who Lives Here?). Toronto: Kids Can Press, 2008.

MacAulay, Kelley, and Bobbie Kalman. *Desert Habitat* (Introducing Habitats). New York: Crabtree, 2008.

Websites

Watch a video on meerkats at: **http://kids.nationalgeographic.com/kids/animals/creaturefeature/meerkat**

Learn more at: **www.sandiegozoo.org/animalbytes/t-meerkat.html**

Index